I sometimes wonder
where I am headed.
Is it enough to just
live for today?
What about tomorrow?
Can I find happiness
with the passing seasons,
or must I begin a new
search once again?

Is there anything wrong
with commitments?
Can they provide new freedom?

I wonder. . .
Do you realize that a
lifetime can be lived
each time we touch,
and our love can be limitless,
if we let it?

PREFACE

These writings are two people's expressions of the development and growth of a deep friendship into a unique love. None of the writings are ever planned—they just happen. Each one is a spontaneous expression of a feeling, a moment or a memory.

The photographs are one man's attempt to capture the feelings and emotions of life. The words and pictures have been blended together in the hope that in sharing a part of our lives, you may gain a little more understanding of your own. We welcome the opportunity to share with you through your own means of creativity and expression.

Love is not only necessary
to begin love,
but necessary to nurture
itself as it grows.
It begins within
and remains throughout.

GROWING. . . TOGETHER

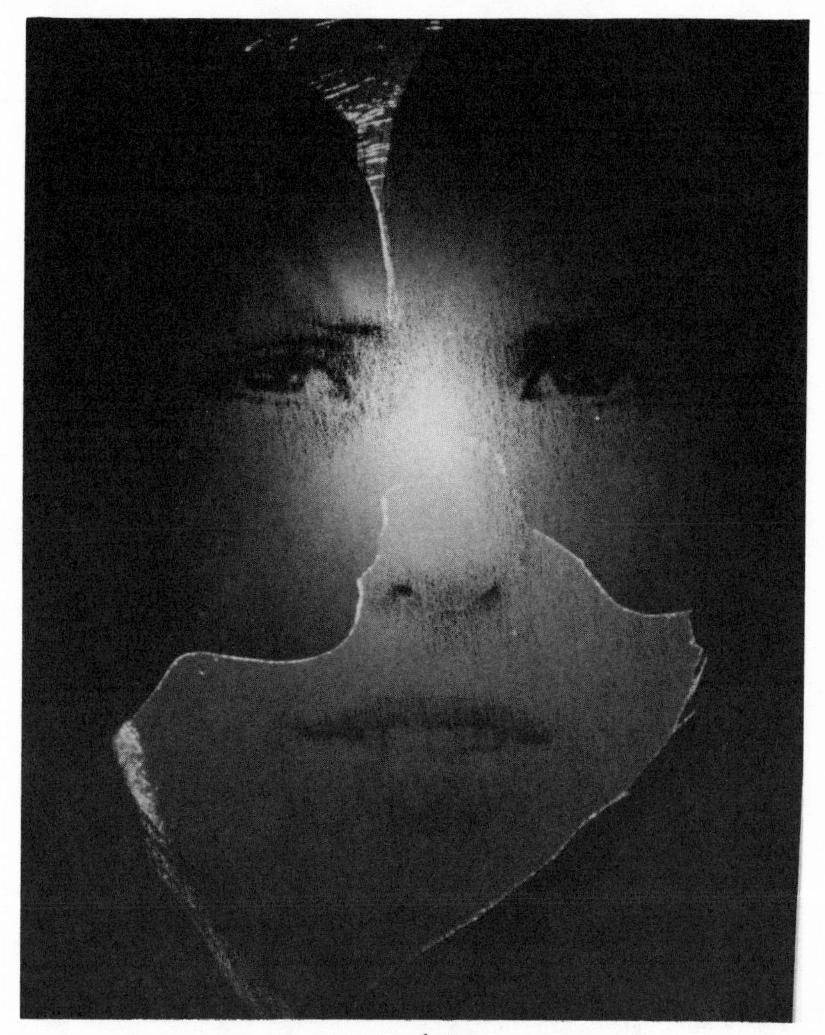

words by
Donni Betts and George Betts
photographs by
Bob Scales

CELESTIAL ARTS
MILLBRAE, CALIFORNIA

231 Adrian Road, Millbrae, California 94030

First Printing, November 1973
Made in the United States of America

Library of Congress Card No.: 73-89890
ISBN: 0-912310-36-7

6 7 8 – 82 81 80 79 78

For our parents,
who, through their own living
have taught us how to love.

A person's dream
is not important
because it does
or does not happen,
but because
it could happen. . .

Another time,
another place,
and we could have made it;
but we were not far enough along,
unaware of an appreciation
of differences,
seeing them only as obstacles.

I wish you the best as we part
for we have given to each other,
even though we may not be
aware of it at this time.

To share my world with you
I must be willing
to be a part of yours.

You say a relationship
which may be fleeting,
with no lasting commitments,
has no meaning, no value.
And I am saddened for you,
and maybe for me. . .
I wonder if you realize
how full your life
could be. . .

You're struggling
and you have
no way to turn.
You've been rejected
and in your aloneness
you must strike out
at anyone
including yourself
to take away the hurt.
I feel so helpless—
wanting you to know
that you are loved,
and with time
you'll be able to begin again.

I don't know which is harder;
saying goodbye
or starting new.
Neither one is easy,
but I need both. . .
Change is part of my growth.

I don't fit anymore.
I did once but
things have changed.
I'll have to begin
searching once more
for that time and place
I can call mine,
but I know someday
that I will have to begin
once more. . .

I face confusion
when I cannot face myself.
My confusion is a detour,
blocking the truth so it
won't hurt me, sheltering
me in a sea of frustration.

Why is it that the ones
with all the answers
have so much trouble
with their own questions?

Once in a while
I am engulfed
by a rare, fleeting feeling
of total spontaneity, creativity.

If the feeling
is not fulfilled
it fades away
and cannot be recaptured.
And somehow I feel sad,
for a part of me
has gone with it.

I sought answers
through adventures
but found peace
from within.

I'm beginning to understand:
no one place will ever
be home for me;
my ties don't run in
that direction.
They have always been
within myself.
But since I've come to
care for you,
you are home too.

I enjoy mornings.
The fog is hazy,
the city is busily
preparing for another day,
and I am reflective,
silently looking
at my life
while drinking a cup of coffee.

I needed to write tonight
for my spoken words
were lost in the noise.

She has everything
but wants more,
and has nothing
for she never
finds peace in herself or the
world around her.

She is a collector
of people and things,
eagerly chosen
for their value,
but forgotten
once purchased.

The collection
continues to grow
but she does not.

He continued to talk,
while she continued
not to listen
while they continued,
so terribly alone,
unaware. . .

I withdrew tonight.
You were irritable
and I didn't want to be
your mental punching bag.

Your silence locks me out,
with only my imagination
for company. . .

When I withdraw,
when I become defensive,
when I act as if I don't care,

These are the times I need you most.

When I feel free
to give of myself to you,
then I know
I am truly free.

A smile is universal, acceptable and inexpensive. . .

I seek the gentle people,
those who radiate beauty
in their own living.

Thank you for listening,
for sharing my doubts and fears,
for accepting me when
I was completely down,
for loving me when
I was lost.

And now that we have met,
we are able to grow,
together.
Our love has given us strength.
Loneliness is no longer our companion
but a reminder of the past and
the traveled miles behind us.

I wonder. . .
Do you see me
as I see me?

There is more in me
for you to discover,
things I like about me
that will delight you
and warm your heart.

Without trusting you,
I cannot give myself.
I can only give "safe" things
which really are not worth giving.

We are not close
for we have not allowed
ourselves
the opportunity
to resolve conflicts.

We remain apart
with only a dream
of a future together.

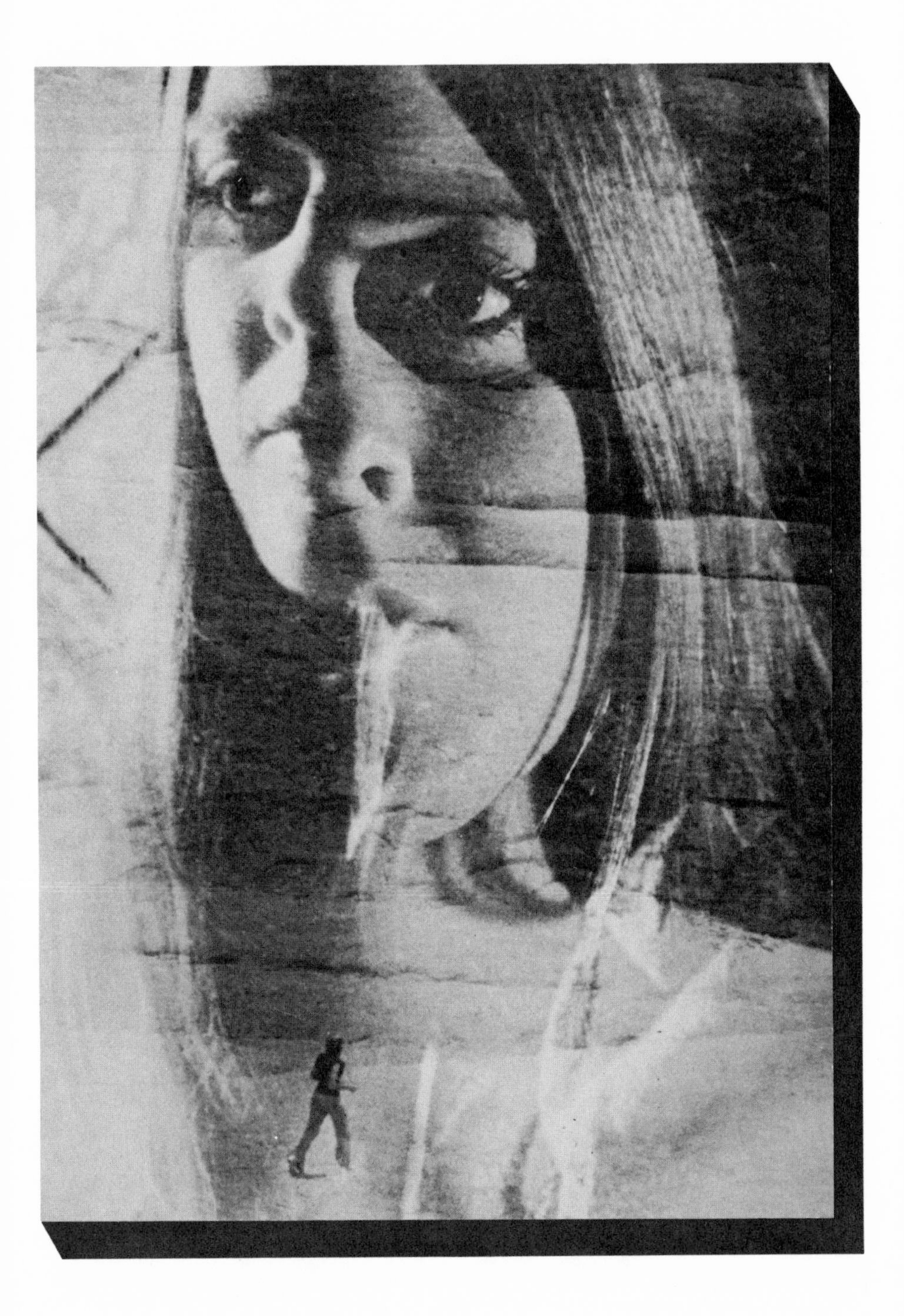

Half of loving is
knowing when
to let go.

I cannot give you your freedom
nor take it from you,
for it has always been yours.

I saw my friend
in the gym today,
and we talked about
the latest basketball scores
and the last heavyweight fight.

Later, when I saw him
walking home in the rain
I offered him a lift,
and we discussed
the weather.

We went to the movie
together tonight,
and afterwards
found ourselves engaged
in a lively argument
over the most talked-about
new movie.

I wonder where people go
to talk about themselves. . .

And in my loneliness
I reach out to no one
for I can't even find me.
I am lost,
  but I am struggling
  to find a way,
and confusion is the beginning. . .

Too much time
can be spent
wondering about life
rather than living it.

Without movement
I am only potential.

We find endless means
of expression
of creativity.
Our ultimate expression
is love,
which is its own creativity.

The sea is never silent,
never still.
She is forever changing,
renewing her shape,
her course.
You and I are like the sea,
for inside we are never silent
nor still,
always seeking new ways to
experience,
new courses to follow.

Did you know I was born
a wanderer?
I went to Egypt
and rode a two-humped camel once,
sitting behind my desk
in fourth grade.
I learned the Highland Fling
and roamed the Scottish Moors
during recess.
I fought off some grizzlies
in the Yukon,
riding in the back
of my daddy's car.
I was even Queen of the World once,
in sixth grade.
Do you want to come and dream with me?

You can be King,
and someday. . .

It's funny. . .
people talk about falling in love.
But I didn't fall in love
with you.
I'm growing in love with you.

Airports consist of
joyful hellos
and tearful goodbyes.
Someday. . .
we'll fly away together.

Bedtime. . .and so lonely to be
so far away from home
and you.
But how precious to know
what it means
to miss you.

When I'm lonely for you,
it doesn't work
to fill my life
with other people.

Loneliness covers me
as the fog drifts in,
covering me, chilled and alone,
with no today and
no signs of tomorrow.
You're gone.
Many days have passed
but I am not aware
of drifting seasons or
changing moods. . .

A friendly smile
or a passing someone
on the street and
I travel back to you
and the memories of
times gone by.

Have I dried up inside
or am I simply preparing
for a new adventure?

How can I ask you
to comfort me
when I can not find
the solace in myself?

Because you are angry
with me
does not mean
that I must
become angry
with you.

You cannot control how
the world handles you,
only how you handle
your world.

It all seems so important now,
but tomorrow you will
feel it less
and later
it will be a memory,
something to guide you,
but not to limit you.

We didn't make it.
Our relationship ended.
We parted as friends
and found ourselves
alone once more,
but that was many years ago.

You have drifted away,
living a life that was
once to be shared with me.

Time has changed so many things.
I no longer think of the bad times,
but appreciate the good ones.

You are still a part of my life,
very important,
my memory.

I am thankful now for what we shared,
for I know it has helped me
to become what I am now.

Our time together
has been short
but it's been long enough
for us to become friends.

I've been to many different places
many different times
but those shared with you are
the ones remembered best.

I've been away a long time now—
nearly a year.
I'm going home soon
and I don't know
what to expect.
So many things change. . .
my old dog died
and the people
across the street moved away.
My favorite TV programs
have probably been replaced
in the inevitable fall review,
and I'm sure my family
will seem somehow different.

I wonder how I've changed. . .

Being far away from you,
I think of you often,
but it is not an empty feeling.
      It is a feeling
            of appreciation.
I remember the uniqueness
            of your expressions,
               the depth
                  of your loving,
                     and the joy and laughter
                        you bring to my world.
And through my memories of you,
                  I am never alone.

A candle's flame seems so small,
yet in the night
how bright it can be.

When I light my candle,
I think of you.

I never did tell you
how important you are to me.
You gave me so much
but I could not tell you.
Somehow I hope you know
that my feelings for you
are stronger
than the words
I could never say.

22

The dreams of a child
are the dreams of the world
unspoiled.

I've heard about what you were
like when you were small.

You've shown me places you
fished with your dad,
taught me things you learned
from him,
given me a sense of belonging
not only to your now,
but to your youth.

I wish I could have known
you then.

Toby was two
when I was four
and together we created
a world of excitement.
He would pull my
wagon in the "Indy 500,"
climb trees with a little help,
and be my companion
in settling the old west.

Toby is only a memory
for me today, for he died
when I was thirteen.
I remember taking him
to the veterinary and
sending him to dog heaven,
but somehow, Toby has never
been forgotten.

You have been her guide
for many years now.
You have watched her learn
what it means
to wait for Santa Claus,
to love a Teddy Bear,
to share a dream world
with a cat named Squeak,
to say good-bye to childhood
and later to her first boyfriend.
You have continued with her
in many directions, and
although your travels
have been long and at times
very tiring, you have helped
her to see that life is
nothing more than what
she believes in.

True motivation
is as mysterious
as life itself.
It must begin within.

Sometimes when I cry
I feel as though it has
just rained,
leaving me fresh,
able to continue
once again. . .

Our hard times
have become pathways
to our happiness.

Loving you is not always easy
but if it were
I probably wouldn't.

I learned something today.
Every time there is conflict
I see a new opportunity
for understanding.

We are free,
a feeling which
is a result
and a beginning.
It is the road
of life,
traveled
only by those who
know that
the greatest risk
is not
to risk at all.

The very close,
the very intimate
moments are usually
few and far between,
but that might be what
makes them so very important.

love takes time
tears
sadness
loneliness
and all the other beautiful
experiences of life.

Our love
is the fantasy
of tomorrow
being lived
today.

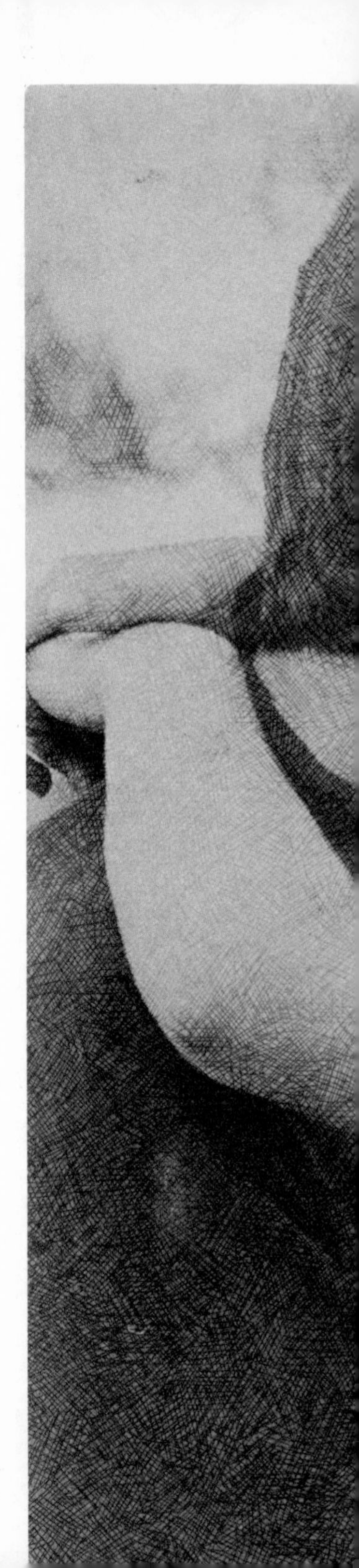

One day in the summer
I hurried home from
an ordinary day at work
to be greeted by you,
a dozen roses
and a poem.

You gave me daisies on
your birthday.

And today you gave me
tulips—for no special reason
at all.

To know life
is to see a thing
in its complexity
and to know it
simply.

In those we love
we find a strength
which gives an added meaning
to our lives,
long after they have gone.

Your silence
reassured me
that expression
becomes complete
when it is shared,
silently.

The butterfly is only beautiful
to those who appreciate the
simple joys of life.

Because you do not expect my love,
I am able to give you everything.

Through our bonds of love
we have discovered the freedom
to grow.

For us,
love is more
than saying hello
and later, goodbye.
Our love did not begin
just to end.
We have built a love
different from any
we have ever experienced
before,
and the only thought
we have about tomorrow
is a continuation
of today.

We have traveled
through loneliness
and sadness
to our place
of understanding,
our place of beauty
where we can continue
growing. . .
together.

George and Donni Betts live near Denver, where George is developing a new creative program for students of the Arvada West High School. Donni is working on a master's degree in psychology, counseling, and guidance at the University of Northern Colorado in Greeley. This is their first book together; George worked alone on the text for Visions of You and My Gift to You.

Bob Scales, the photographer for this and for George's previous two books, left the editorship of a newspaper in Greeley, last year to return to teaching at the junior high school in Kit Carson, Colorado. At the same time he has been developing his skills in creative photography. He also coaches football, basketball, wrestling, and track, and teaches language arts.

George is a member of the Jefferson County, Colorado and National Education Associations.

Bob is a member of the National Education Association and the Photographic Society of America.